HAL LEONARD GUITAR METHOD

CHRISTIAN GUITAR

BY CHAD JOHNSON

T0084237

PLAYBACK+
Speed • Pitch • Balance • Loop

To access audio visit:
www.halleonard.com/mylibrary

Enter Code
1237-1493-6247-7577

Recording Credits:

Vocals: Tonia Emerich and Jim Reith   Keyboards: Warren Wiegratz

Guitars: Doug Boduch   Drums: Scott Schroedl

Bass: Tom McGirr

Recorded, mixed, and mastered by Jim Reith at Beathouse Music, Milwaukee, WI

ISBN 978-1-4234-1605-0

HAL•LEONARD®
CORPORATION

7777 W. BLUEMOUND RD. P.O. BOX 13819 MILWAUKEE, WI 53213

Visit Hal Leonard Online at
www.halleonard.com

INTRODUCTION

Welcome to the *Hal Leonard Christian Guitar Method*. In this book, you'll learn guitar by playing popular Christian songs. If you're brand new to the instrument, don't fret. We're going to start from ground zero and work our way through some more intermediate/advanced concepts later in the book. What's more, you'll get to hear your newfound skills at work in several classic songs right away.

The material in this book is suited equally for acoustic or electric guitar. If you have one of each, try playing through the examples with both instruments. Though they both have six strings and are essentially played the same, there is quite a difference in feel between the two, and it's a good idea to get acclimated to both early on in your development if possible. If you only have one or the other, don't sweat it. Making the transition later on (if you choose to do so) shouldn't be too problematic.

Ready to go? Take out your axe (that's slang for "guitar") and let's get started!

TABLATURE AND CHORD GRIDS

Guitar players have long used a number system called *tablature*, or "tab" for short, as a means of guitar notation. Tablature consists of six horizontal lines, each representing a string on the guitar. The top line represents the high E string (the thinnest string), second line the B string, third line the G string, and so on. A number on the line indicates the fret number at which you play the note.

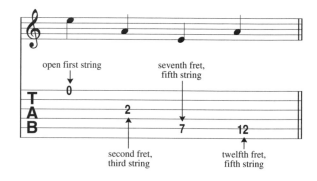

open first string

seventh fret, fifth string

second fret, third string

twelfth fret, fifth string

Some examples make use of *chord grids*. Here's a look at how they're read. The six vertical lines represent the six strings on the guitar, from low to high (left to right).

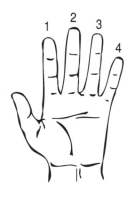

An "x" indicates that the string is to muted or not played.

An "o" indicates that the string is to be played open.

This thick line represents the nut.

Dots indicate where to place your fingers.

Horizontal lines represent frets.

These numbers indicate which fingers to use.

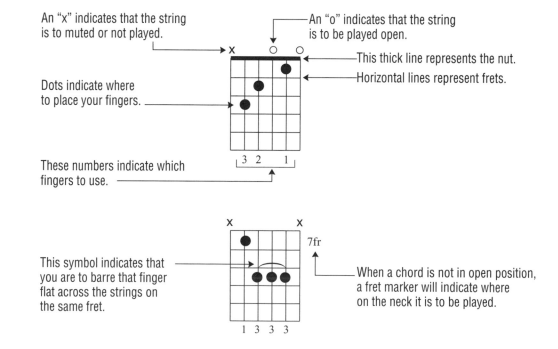

This symbol indicates that you are to barre that finger flat across the strings on the same fret.

When a chord is not in open position, a fret marker will indicate where on the neck it is to be played.

ABOUT THE AUDIO 🔊

The audio includes demonstrations of all the examples in this book. The corresponding track number for each song or example is listed below the audio icon. All of the songs in the book also include a separate play-along track with the featured guitar part removed. On the demo tracks, the featured guitar part is always on the right channel.

PRELIMINARIES

Before we dive right in, let's get familiar with a few basics you need to know.

PARTS OF A GUITAR

Let's learn the names for all your guitar's parts. The electric and acoustic guitar share many of the same basic parts, but there are a few differences.

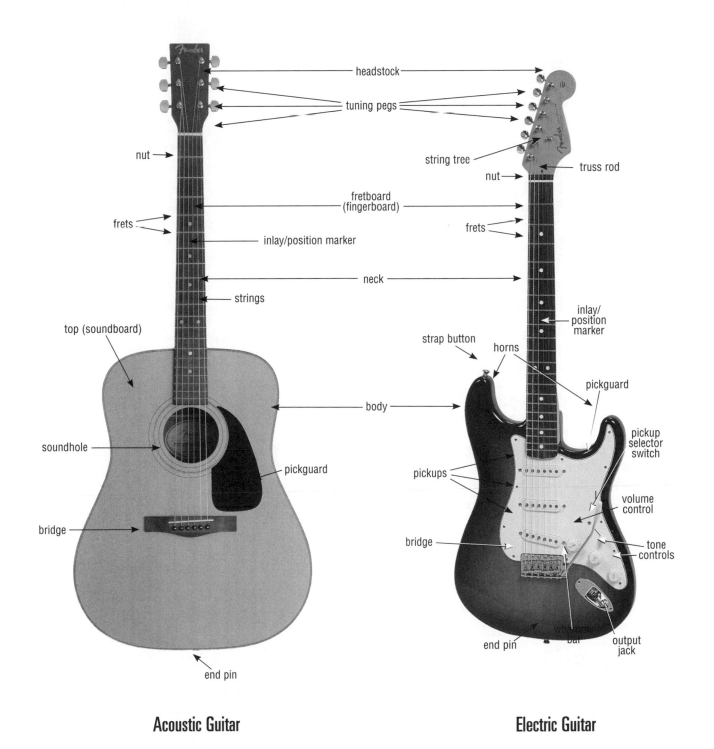

Acoustic Guitar   **Electric Guitar**

HOLDING THE INSTRUMENT

Sitting

When sitting, most players prefer to rest their guitar on their right leg. Allow the back of the guitar's body to rest against your rib cage and keep it in place with your right forearm. Some people like to use a foot stool to raise the leg and increase the stability, but unless the guitar is terribly heavy, this isn't usually necessary.

Standing

Standing requires the use of a strap, which should be adjustable so you can find a comfortable height. You'll most likely have to go through a bit of a trial-and-error to find a comfortable playing position. The neck should be at an angle, as this will make the job of fretting much easier. Your strap should be completely supporting the weight of the guitar, so there's no need to anchor your right forearm against the body.

TUNING

Getting your instrument in tune is very important. If it's out of tune, it won't sound right—no matter how well you play. There are a few different ways to tune: using an electronic tuner, tuning to reference pitches, or tuning by ear.

The six open strings of the guitar are tuned to the following notes, from low to high: **E-A-D-G-B-E**. The strings are numbered as well from 1 to 6, with 6 being the thickest, lowest-pitched string.

An **electronic tuner** is a device that you plug your guitar into. When you play a string, it tells you which note it is and whether you're sharp (too high in pitch) or flat (too low in pitch). This is probably the easiest method of tuning. You simply play a string and adjust the pitch of the string using the tuning pegs until the tuner indicates that you're in tune.

Tuning with **reference pitches** requires a little more attention on your part. In this instance, you're given the pitch of each open string and you have to match that pitch by adjusting your tuning pegs. You're forced to use your ear here. This is invaluable training, as the development of your ear is critical to becoming an accomplished musician. The pitches can be given to you by another guitar player, a piano, or, you can listen to audio track 1 to hear the pitches.

 Tuning pitches

TRACK 1

Tuning **by ear** is similar to using reference pitches. In fact, tuning with reference pitches is actually tuning by ear, but usually the term "tuning by ear" refers to tuning your instrument "to itself." In order to use this method, you'll need to try to obtain just one reference pitch. If you can get the low E string (sixth string), that's best.

Now, use the following procedure:

- Play fret 5 of the sixth string; this will produce the note A. While letting that note ring, play the open fifth string. While both strings ring, reach over with the picking hand and tune the fifth string to match the A pitch.

- Play fret 5 of the fifth string; this will produce the note D. While letting that note ring, play the open fourth string. Tune the fourth string to match the D pitch.

- Play fret 5 of the fourth string; this will produce the note G. While letting that note ring, play the open third string. Tune the third string to match the G pitch.

- Play fret 4 of the third string (this is the only exception); this will produce the note B. While letting that note ring, play the open second string. Tune the second string to match the B pitch.

- Play fret 5 of the second string; this will produce the note E. While letting that note ring, play the open first string. Tune the first string to match the E pitch.

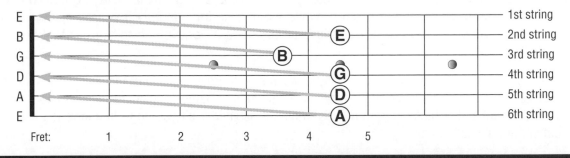

TUNING TIPS

- It's best to tune *up* to pitch rather than tune down. If you need to tune a string that's too high (sharp), first bring it down below the target pitch and then tune back up. Your guitar will hold its tuning better with this method.

- Listen for "beats" to help you tune. Beats are the result of two pitches being slightly out of tune. The result is a wavering sound. The more beats you hear, the more out of tune you are. As you progress closer to being in tune, the beats will slow down and eventually stop altogether.

- Be patient. Tuning takes practice. And while electronic tuners are nice for convenience, they can become a crutch. It's best to learn to tune by ear first before solely relying on electronic tuners. Besides, there are bound to be many times when you don't have a tuner around, and it's then you'll be thankful for the time you took to train your ear.

TECHNICAL TIPS

Right Hand

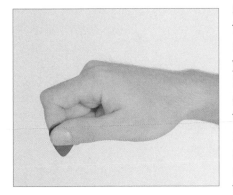

Some players prefer to use their fingers to pluck the strings, but the majority of players prefer to use a **pick** (or *plectrum*). Grasp the pick between your thumb and first finger. Your thumb should be somewhere between the tip and first knuckle of your first finger. Hold the pick so that it strikes the strings at a slight downward angle. This will make for a more efficient picking motion. You should be holding it tightly enough so that it doesn't constantly come free, but not so tight as to cut off your circulation!

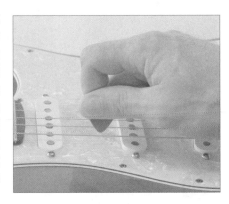

Left Hand

The fingers of your left hand should be curved, as if holding a ball. (There are a few exceptions to this rule that you'll run into eventually, but don't worry about that at this point.) Use your thumb to apply pressure on the back of the neck when fretting, so as to facilitate the pressure needed to depress the string.

When fretting, it's best to actually fret near the front of the fret space towards the bridge rather than the middle. The farther you move back in the fret space, the more you risk creating *fret buzz*: an unpleasant sound created by a string rattling against a fret.

CHAPTER 1: OPEN CHORDS

Guitar playing often falls into one of two basic, broad categories: *lead* and *rhythm*. Playing lead usually involves playing one note at a time (as in a guitar solo), while playing rhythm usually involves playing several notes at once. Rhythm playing occupies most of a guitarist's time, so it's a good place to start. (Most people also find rhythm a bit easier than lead.)

When playing rhythm, you'll spend most of your time playing **chords**. A *chord* is a group of three or more notes played at the same time. There are all different kinds of chords with all different kinds of names, including major, minor, seventh, and so on; each one sounds different and evokes different moods within the listener. We're going to first look at a few *major* chords, which are the most commonly used of all.

On guitar, an *open chord* is a chord that uses one or more open (unfretted) strings. These are usually the easiest to play, and they sound great. Let's try an E chord to begin with. First get your left-hand fingers into position as shown on the chord grid. Remember to press firmly with each finger. Once you're all set, strum through all six strings with the pick.

TRACK 2

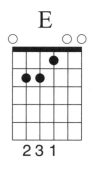

E

2 3 1

Now let's try another chord. This one is an A chord. Notice that only five strings are played for this chord.

TRACK 3

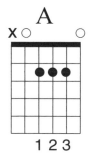

A

1 2 3

Here are a few things to keep in mind when playing these open chords:

- Make sure all the notes in the chord are ringing out clearly. This can be accomplished by plucking each string individually after you've fretted the chord. If one note sounds muted or muffled, chances are one of your other fingers is touching the string or you're fretting too lightly.

- You don't want strings ringing out that aren't supposed to. The "x" on the chord grid indicates that the string should not be sounding at all. In the case of an A chord, for example, you don't want the low E (sixth) string to ring. There are two ways to accomplish this: 1) Bring your left-hand thumb just over the top of the neck to lightly touch the sixth string, deadening it. 2) Begin your strum from the fifth string.

  I highly recommend the deadening method, as the second method requires an impractical amount of precision when actively strumming. If you get into the habit of deadening the strings that you're not playing, you can strum away and not have to worry about avoiding certain strings. This may require a slight adjustment to your typical fretting technique, but nothing drastic.

- Don't get discouraged! Your fingers are going to get a little sore at first. As you play more, you'll build up calluses on your fingertips, and the soreness will go away.

- Fingernails on your left (fretting) hand are not your friends! Keeping them trimmed will make playing chords much easier.

Here's a D chord. You're only playing the top four strings on this one.

TRACK 4

Now try a G chord.

TRACK 5

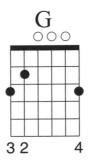

Now let's take a look at our first *minor* chord, A minor. You'll notice that this chord sounds different from the earlier major chords. Generally, it's said that major chords have a happy or bright sound, while minor chords have a sad or dark sound.

TRACK 6

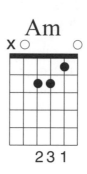

Am

2 3 1

Here's another popular minor chord: E minor.

TRACK 7

Em

2 3

MORE CHORD FACTS

- The "root" of the chord is the note from which the chord gets its name. It's usually the lowest note. So, "A" is the root of an A chord.

- The lowercase "m" on a minor chord's symbol is known as the *suffix* of a chord name. The distinction of major, minor, etc., refers to a chord's *quality*.

- Notice that the chord symbol for a major chord is simply an uppercase letter with no suffix (e.g., "E" stands for E major).

- The most common type of chord is the *triad*, which has three different notes. All of the chords we've learned so far have been triads. (Note: Even though the chords involve more than three strings, they're still triads. Some notes are simply being used twice in the chord; there are still only three *different* notes.)

- Major and minor chords with the same root only differ by one note.

CHAPTER 2: READING MUSIC

Although it's not essential by any means to be an expert music reader in order to learn the guitar, it is necessary to cover a few fundamentals. In this chapter we'll look at the basics of music notation so you'll be better prepared to make sense of the examples throughout this book. This will also make it easier to further your musical knowledge and communicate with other musicians.

THE STAFF

Music is written on a group of five horizontal lines called a *staff*. The different lines (and the spaces between them) are assigned different musical *notes*. The notes proceed in pitch from low to high as you move up the staff.

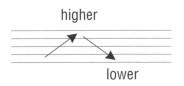
higher

lower

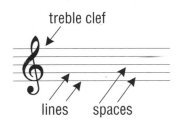
treble clef

lines   spaces

In music we name each note with a letter from the alphabet, but only using the letters A through G. A symbol at the left of the staff, known as a *clef*, tells us which note names are assigned to which lines and spaces on the staff. Guitar music (and a good deal of music for other instruments) is written on the *treble clef*.

On the treble clef staff, the notes are arranged as follows: the lines, from low to high, are assigned the notes E, G, B, D, and F; the spaces, from low to high, are assigned the notes F, A, C, and E. The lines are easily memorized by using the phrase "**E**very **G**ood **B**oy **D**oes **F**ine," while the spaces spell the word "**FACE**."

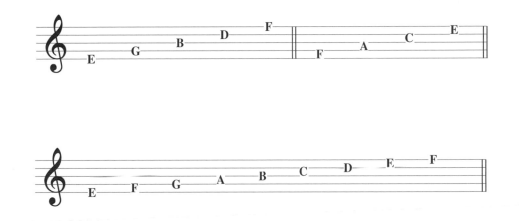

Notice that, when taken together, the notes simply climb through the alphabet, starting over again at A after reaching G.

ACCIDENTALS

Though there are only seven note names in the musical alphabet (A through G), there are actually twelve different pitches available to us. This is because there are certain notes that fall in the cracks between the seven notes. These notes are accessed via the use of *accidentals*. There are two types of accidental symbols you'll often come across: the sharp and the flat.

The **sharp** symbol (♯), which resembles an italic number sign, is used to raise a pitch one half step. A half step is the distance of one fret on the guitar.

The **flat** symbol (♭), which resembles a lowercase b, is used to lower a pitch one half step.

Another symbol you'll see in conjunction with these accidentals is the **natural** symbol (♮). This symbol cancels out a previous sharp or flat sign, returning the note to its "natural" state.

There are two spots in the musical alphabet where notes don't exist "in the cracks:" between E and F, and between B and C. This is why there are twelve notes in all: seven "natural" notes and five notes "in between."

RHYTHM

The rhythms in music tell us how long to play each note. Every note that appears on the staff is distinguished by a certain rhythm.

Measures

The staff is divided into *measures* by *bar lines*. Each measure is made up of a certain number of rhythmic beats. The most common number of beats in a measure is four.

Time Signature

The time signature is a set of numbers that looks like a fraction at the beginning of a piece and lets the performer know how the rhythm is organized. The top number tells the performer how many beats are in a measure; the bottom number tells what kind of note is counted as the beat. The most common time signature by far is 4/4.

Note Values

Notes on the staff look different depending upon their assigned rhythm. There are many different rhythmic values, but here are the most common:

A *whole note* lasts for four beats or a whole measure.

A *half note* lasts for two beats or half a measure.

A *quarter note* lasts for one beat, or one quarter of a measure.

An *eighth note* lasts for half a beat, or one eighth of a measure.

When several eighth notes appear in a row, they're joined together by *beams* to make reading them easier.

So, the 4/4 time signature tells us that there are four beats in a measure (top number), and the quarter note (bottom number) gets the beat.

Rests

A *rest* tells the performer to be silent for a specific amount of time. For every rhythmic note, there is a corresponding rest.

Notes		Equivalent Rests	
Whole note	𝅝	Whole rest	▬
Half note	𝅗𝅥	Half rest	▬
Quarter note	𝅘𝅥	Quarter rest	𝄽
Eighth note	𝅘𝅥𝅮	Eighth rest	𝄾

Ties and Dots

A *tie* combines the value of two notes. The first note is played and sustained through the rhythmic value of the second note.

A *dot* increases a note's rhythmic value by 50 percent. So, a dotted half note equals one half note plus one quarter note. A dotted quarter note is equal to one quarter note plus one eighth note, etc.

Listen to the audio example to hear these devices in action.

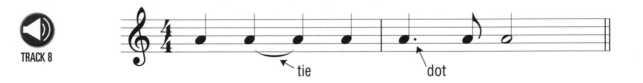

TRACK 8

tie   dot

Tempo

The *tempo* of a piece of music refers to how fast or slow the beat is. It's measured in beats per minute (bpm) and is indicated at the beginning of the music. The higher the number, the faster the tempo. Occasionally, descriptive words (Fast, Moderately, etc.) are used in place of or in conjunction with bpm directions.

Moderately 𝅘𝅥 = 100

CHAPTER 3: STRUMMING

Strumming is one of the most important techniques you'll ever learn as a guitar player. In fact, in the contemporary Christian genre, you'll most likely spend more time strumming than anything else on the guitar. Developing a strong strumming technique will allow you to create a solid sense of rhythm with your playing, which will encourage listeners to move and sing along!

In this book, we'll use *chord slashes* to indicate strumming rhythms for chords. These are shaped like long, slanted boxes as opposed to normal, circular notes.

When strumming, we make use of *downstrokes* and *upstrokes*. They're indicated in the music by symbols: (⊓) = downstroke, (∨) = upstroke. Upstrokes are usually reserved for rhythms of an eighth note or faster. Let's start out with a few downstroke exercises to get acquainted with reading chord slash notation. We'll use the chords we learned in Chapter 1. If you're having trouble remembering the rhythmic values of notes, refer back to Chapter 2, and listen to the audio example to clear up any uncertainty.

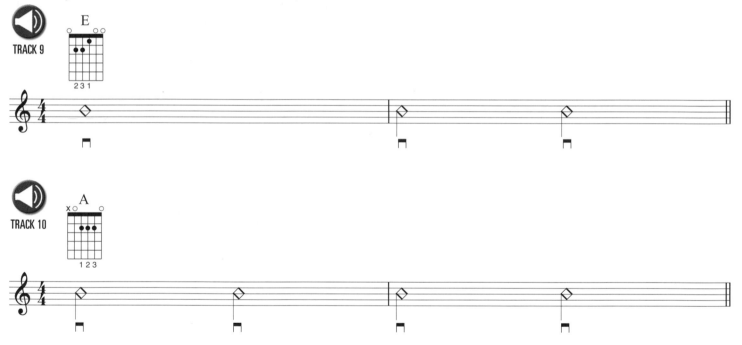

Here we see a half rest. When this occurs, simply allow the side of your picking hand to touch the strings, which will stop them from ringing.

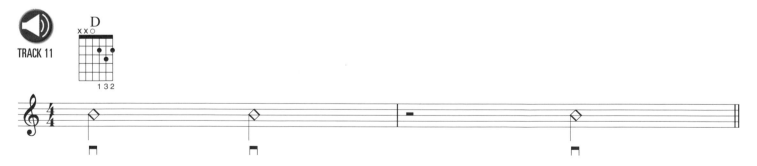

If you're having trouble following along, try the following:

- **Count aloud:** Try counting the beats (say "one, two, three, four") out loud along with the music.

- **Tap your foot:** It also helps to involve your body physically in the counting process. Tapping your foot or bobbing your head will work well in this regard.

- **Prepare:** Make sure you bring your picking hand up and prepare for your next downstroke in plenty of time.

Now let's bring in some quarter notes. This means we'll be strumming on each beat.

The lines and dots at the beginning and end of this example are *repeat signs*. They tell the performer to repeat the music that's enclosed within them. If the first repeat sign is missing (the one with the dots to the right), then you are to repeat from the beginning of the entire song.

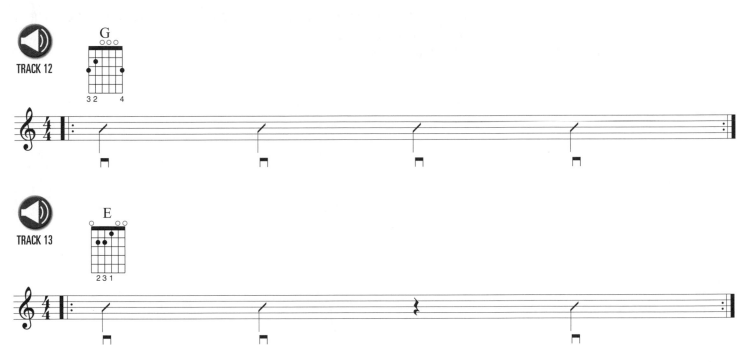

Now let's add in some eighth notes. When counting eighth notes, we say "and" in between the beats: "one and two and three and four and." For the strums that fall on the "ands" in between the beats you'll use an upstroke. You should always use downstrokes and upstrokes this way; the downstroke is used for the strong downbeat, and the upstroke is used for the weak upbeat (the "in betweens").

Look at the strum directions closely in these following examples.

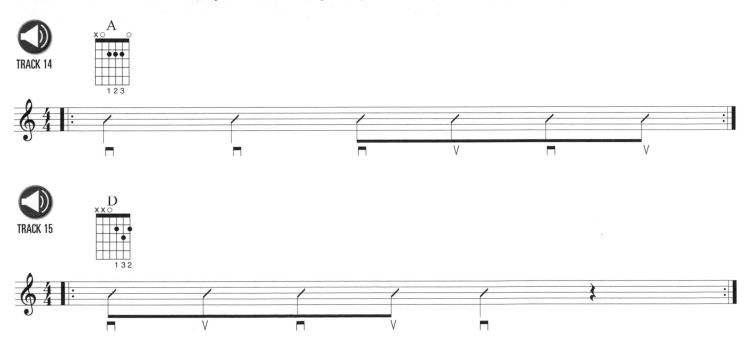

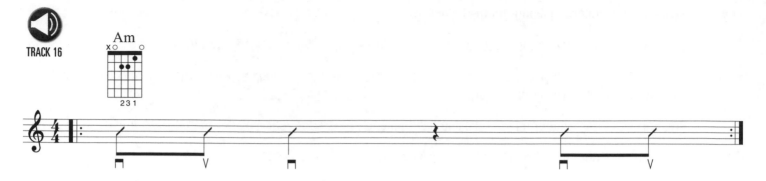

CHANGING CHORDS

When learning to transition between two chords, start out very slowly. What you *don't* want to do is chug along on one chord in tempo, then pause, and then pick the tempo back up for the next chord. Slow the tempo way down at the beginning and increase only when you're able to change chords without dropping a beat.

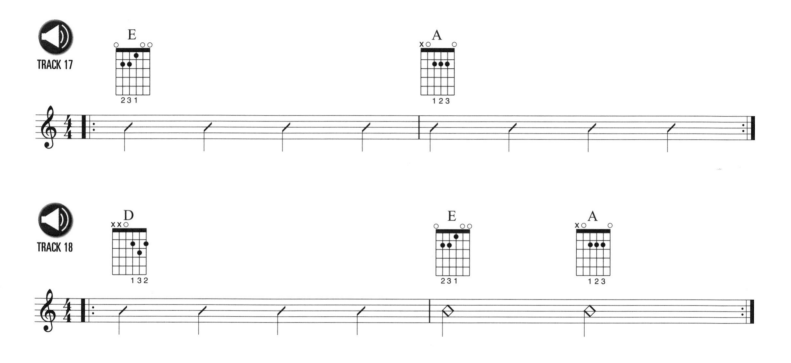

CHORD-CHANGING TIPS

Common Tones

A *common tone* is a note (or notes) shared between two different chords. When you're able to keep one or more fingers down during a chord transition, the result will be a much smoother sound. Notice in the following example how your second finger can remain planted when moving from G to Em.

Try looking for common tones with any group of chords you encounter.

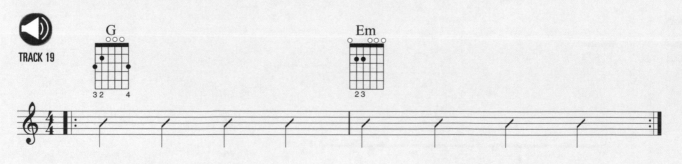

The Open Strum

The second method we'll look at is the *open strum*. This technique is often used when you have to change chords during an eighth-note strum pattern. You simply use the last "and" of the measure to lift your left hand and prepare it for the next chord. While you're doing this, simply strum the open strings (try to strum just the top few) with an upstroke to keep the momentum going.

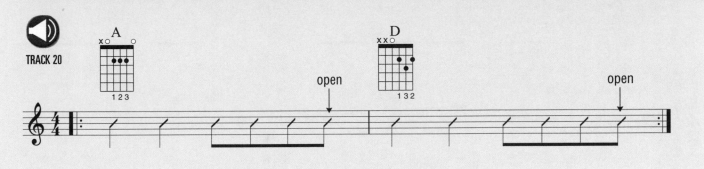

Now let's hear these concepts in some real songs.

CREATE IN ME A CLEAN HEART

LORD, I LIFT YOUR NAME ON HIGH

Lord, I lift Your name on high,

Lord, I love to sing Your prais - es. I'm so glad You're in my

life. I'm so glad You came to save us.

Words and Music by RICK FOUNDS
© 1989 Maranatha Praise, Inc. (admin. by Music Services) (ASCAP)
All Rights Reserved   Used by Permission

COME, NOW IS THE TIME TO WORSHIP

CHAPTER 4: MORE OPEN CHORDS

ow that you're getting the basics down, let's expand your vocabulary of open chords. These chords will require you to stretch the fingers of your fretting hand a bit more, which will feel a bit awkward at first. Don't sweat it, though. With consistent practice it will eventually become second nature!

Let's try a C chord.

TRACK 27

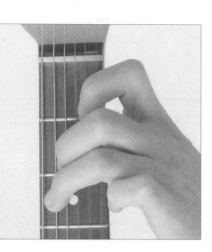

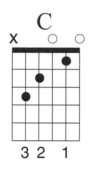

C

3 2 1

Now try D minor.

TRACK 28

Dm

2 3 1

The last open chord we'll look at is B7. This is a different type of chord from a triad called a *seventh chord*. Seventh chords are basically a triad with one added note. Depending on the context, they can sound kind of bluesy or more tense than a major chord.

TRACK 29

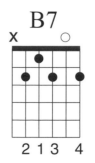

B7

2 1 3 4

Let's hear some of these new chords in action.

I COULD SING OF YOUR LOVE FOREVER

FOREVER

19

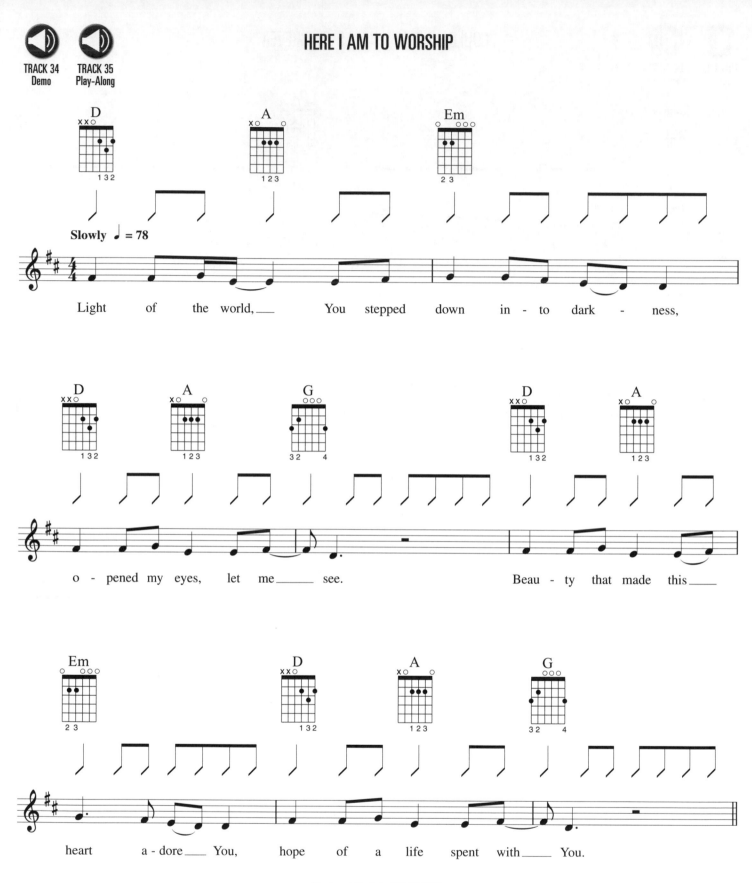

Words and Music by TIM HUGHES
© 2001 THANKYOU MUSIC (PRS)
Admin. Worldwide by EMI CMG PUBLISHING excluding Europe which is Admin. by kingswaysongs.com
All Rights Reserved   Used by Permission

OH LORD, YOU'RE BEAUTIFUL

Words and Music by CHRIS TOMLIN, JESSE REEVES and ED CASH
© 2004 WORSHIPTOGETHER.COM SONGS (ASCAP), sixsteps Music (ASCAP) and ALLETROP MUSIC (BMI)
WORSHIPTOGETHER.COM SONGS and sixsteps Music Admin. by EMI CMG PUBLISHING
ALLETROP MUSIC Admin. by MUSIC SERVICES
All Rights Reserved   Used by Permission

CHAPTER 5: SCALES

A *scale* is a collection of notes that together suggest a certain musical mood or tonality. Some scales sound happy, others sound sad, while some others may sound bluesy, bright, or mysterious. The two most commonly used scales in modern music are the *major scale* and the *minor scale*.

We use scales to make melodies, and to play solos. They're everywhere in music. Every melody you hear, be it vocal or instrumental, is built upon a certain scale.

THE MAJOR SCALE

The major scale is the most important scale you could ever know. Every other scale is described in relation to it. It contains seven different notes and can be built upon any root (C, D, G, etc.).

Let's take a look at a C major scale. We'll play it in quarter notes. Check the tab to make sure you're in the right spot. Start off very slowly; it will take a bit of time to develop the needed synchronization between your left and right hands. Playing single notes requires a little more precision than playing chords.

TRACK 40

C major scale

One of the great things about the guitar is that you can play the same notes at many different spots on the neck. This same scale can be played without using any open strings, as found below. Pay attention to the left-hand fingering given, and listen to how the tone is slightly different than when using some open strings.

TRACK 41

C major scale

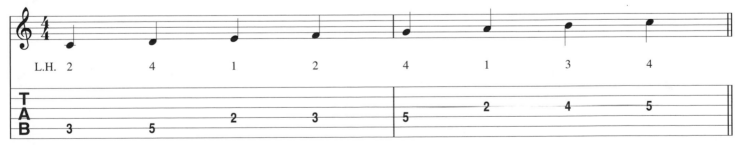

Because this scale shape doesn't contain any open strings, it's a *moveable* shape. This means that you can move the same shape to any root along the same string, and you'll be playing a major scale from a different root. If we move the shape up two frets, for instance, we'll be playing a D major scale.

TRACK 42

D major scale

THE MINOR SCALE

Whereas the major scale sounds happy and bright, the minor scale sounds sad and dark. The minor scale contains the same notes as the major scale, but three of them are lowered by one half step: the 3rd, 6th, and 7th notes.

Let's take a look at a C minor scale. Notice how much darker it sounds compared to the C major scale.

TRACK 43

C minor scale

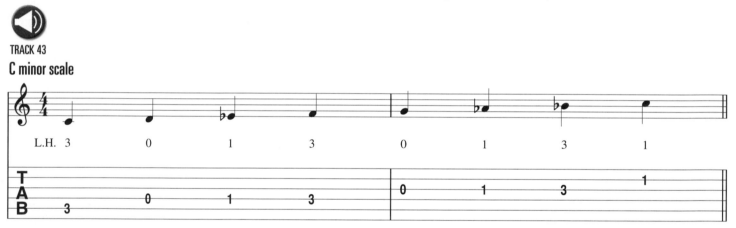

We can make a moveable shape for the minor scale as well. Here's the C minor scale again, this time in a moveable shape (no open strings).

TRACK 44

C minor scale

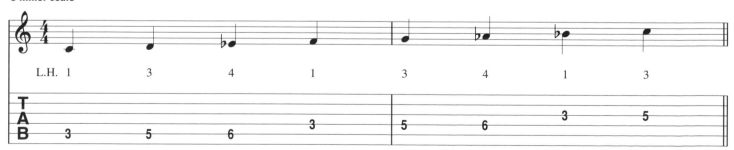

By moving up two frets, we're playing a D minor scale.

TRACK 45

D minor scale

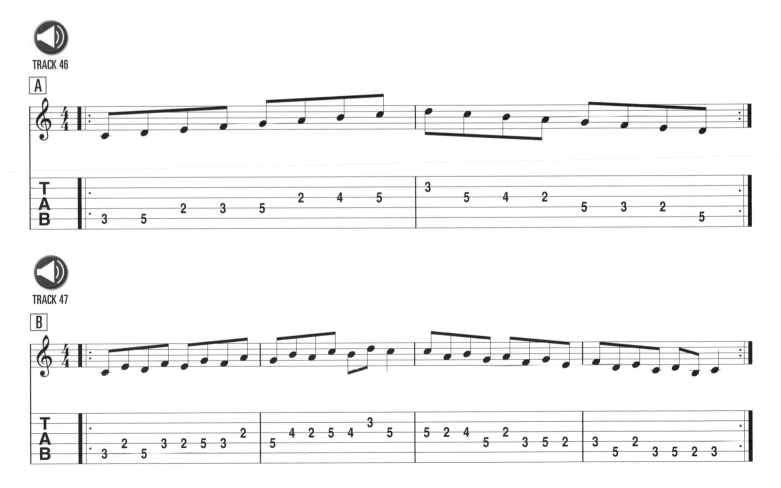

SCALE EXERCISES

Playing scale exercises is a wonderful way to improve your hand-to-hand coordination as well as your fretting-hand agility. Play these at a slow tempo to start, and make it your goal to match the audio example.

> You'll notice that these exercises contain a few notes higher or lower than the scale shapes we learned. In practical application, a scale can cover the entire range of an instrument. The shapes we learned spanned one *octave* (the distance between one note and a higher note of the same name).

Major Scale Exercises

TRACK 46

TRACK 47

TRACK 48

C

Minor Scale Exercises

TRACK 49

A

TRACK 50

B

Now let's play a few familiar melodies built from these scales. The chord symbols are shown as well if you want to try strumming along.

AWESOME GOD

Our God is an awe-some God; He reigns from heav-en a-bove with wis-dom, pow'r and love. Our God is an awe-some God!

*See Appendix

Words and Music by RICH MULLINS
Copyright © 1988 by Universal Music - MGB Songs
International Copyright Secured   All Rights Reserved

FATHER I ADORE YOU

TRACK 54 Demo TRACK 55 Play-Along

Moderately slow ♩ = 86

Fa - ther, I a - dore You. Lay my life be - fore You, how I love You.

Words and Music by TERRY COELHO STROM
© 1972 (Renewed 2000) CCCM MUSIC (Administered by MARANATHA! MUSIC c/o THE COPYRIGHT COMPANY, Nashville, TN) and
MARANATHA! MUSIC (Administered by THE COPYRIGHT COMPANY, Nashville, TN)
All Rights Reserved   International Copyright Secured   Used by Permission

MORE PRECIOUS THAN SILVER

TRACK 56 Demo TRACK 57 Play-Along

Moderately ♩ = 92

Lord, You are more pre - cious than sil - ver. Lord, You are more cost - ly than gold. Lord, You are more beau - ti - ful than dia - monds, and noth - ing I de - sire com - pares with You.

Words and Music by LYNN DESHAZO
© 1982 Integrity's Hosanna! Music/ASCAP
c/o Integrity Media, Inc., 1000 Cody Road, Mobile, AL 36695
All Rights Reserved   International Copyright Secured   Used by Permission

28

CHAPTER 6: MORE STRUMMING

In this chapter, we're going to greatly expand our strumming options by introducing a concept known as syncopation. To syncopate means to place a stress on a weak beat. This can really make your strum patterns come to life and infuse a newfound energy into your rhythm playing. In order to do this, we're going to make use of a concept called a ghost stroke to purposefully miss certain strums.

Let's first look at a normal eighth-note strumming pattern. Remember to strum down on the downbeats and up on the upbeats (the "ands" in between the beats).

TRACK 58

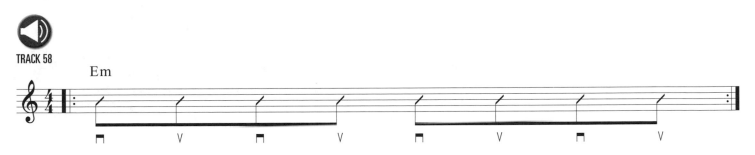

Now we're going to add some syncopation by "missing" one of the strums. Everything is the same, but on beat 3 we won't make contact with the strings on the downstroke. Your right hand should still be moving up and down at a constant rate, but you'll simply bring your hand out slightly for the ghost stroke on beat 3. Notice how the rhythm suddenly comes alive!

TRACK 59

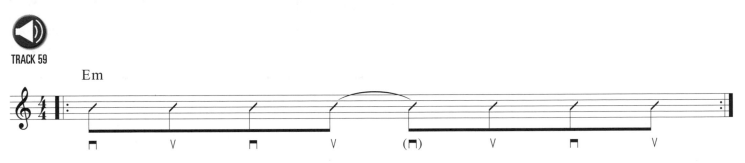

Let's take a look at another example. Here's the non-syncopated version.

TRACK 60

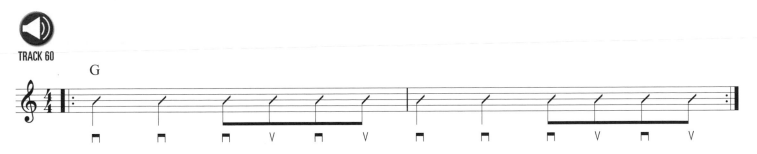

Now we're placing the ghost stroke on beat 1 of measure 2. Pay close attention to the picking directions. Your right hand should still be moving in steady time.

TRACK 61

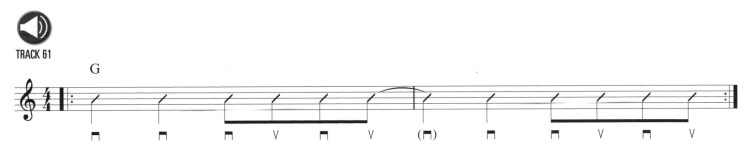

Here are a couple more syncopated examples. Follow the picking directions closely!

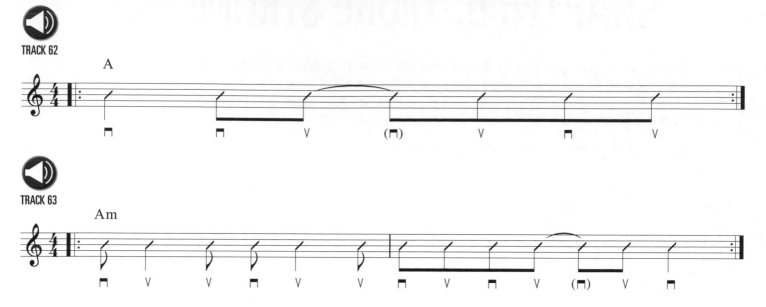

OK. Let's take a look at some of these syncopated patterns at work in some real songs.

BLESSED BE YOUR NAME

OPEN THE EYES OF MY HEART

O-pen the eyes of my heart, Lord,

o-pen the eyes of my heart. I want to see You,

I want to see You.

Words and Music by PAUL BALOCHE
© 1997 Integrity's Hosanna! Music/ASCAP
c/o Integrity Media, Inc., 1000 Cody Road, Mobile, AL 36695
All Rights Reserved   International Copyright Secured   Used by Permission

THE HEART OF WORSHIP

I'm com-ing back to the heart of wor - ship, and it's all a-bout You,

all a-bout You, Je - sus. I'm sor-ry, Lord, for the thing I've made it, when it's

all a-bout You, all a-bout You, Je - sus.

Words and Music by MATT REDMAN
© 1998 THANKYOU MUSIC (PRS)
Admin. Worldwide by EMI CMG PUBLISHING excluding Europe which is Admin. by kingswaysongs.com
All Rights Reserved   Used by Permission

CHAPTER 7: MOVEABLE CHORD SHAPES

In Chapter 5, we learned about the subject of moveable shapes as it applies to scales. Well, it can also apply to chords. Any chord that is played without the use of an open string can be moved anywhere on the neck to another root. In this chapter, we're going to look at one very practical application of this concept: the *power chord*.

THE POWER CHORD

While a triad contains three different notes, the power chord contains only two. On its own, it is neither major nor minor, because the note that it lacks is the one that's responsible for the major/minor quality. Power chords sound big and spacious. Because of this, they're commonly used more in rock genres and are therefore partial to the electric guitar.

Although power chords contain only two different notes, they're most commonly fingered on the guitar with three strings. This doubles the root note an octave higher and lends to the bigness of their sound. Some distortion is often used on power chords to enhance their "rock 'n' roll" sound.

The chord symbol for a power chord is an uppercase letter and a "5" as a suffix. Here's a G5 chord, which is built from the sixth string.

 TRACK 70

Since there are no open strings involved, we can move this shape anywhere up and down the sixth string to play power chords from different roots.

 TRACK 71

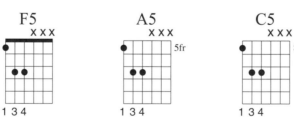

Now here's a C5 built from the fifth string.

 TRACK 72

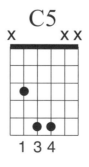

32

Just as with the sixth-string form, this form can be moved anywhere on the neck to play other power chords with fifth-string roots.

TRACK 73

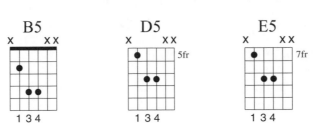

Let's look at a few examples using moveable power chords. (Note: the "X" slash that appears in some of these examples is a *muted strum*. Simply release pressure with your left hand but keep the fingers lightly on the strings while you strum. The result will be a percussive clicking sound.)

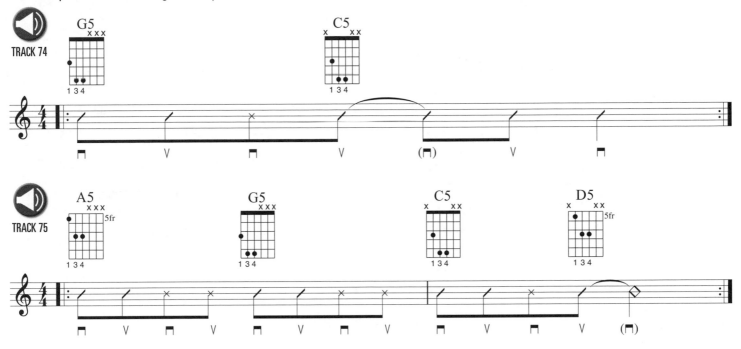

Of course, you can also play power chords using open strings. The following examples demonstrate this with open E5 and A5 shapes.

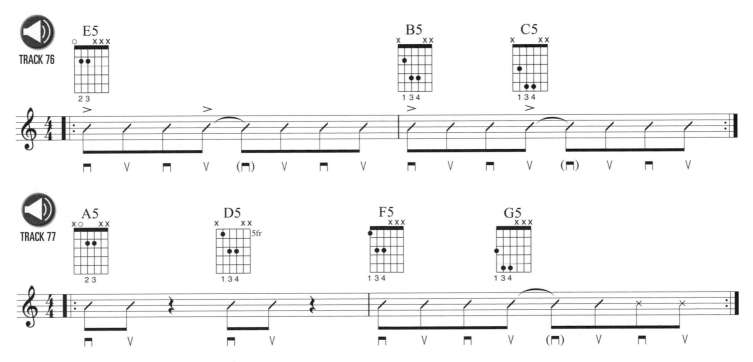

Note: The little "greater than" symbols (>) you see in track 76 are called *accent marks*. They tell the performer to play that chord or note more strongly (louder and with more force) than the other notes.

Now here are some power chords at work in real songs.

YOU ARE MY KING
(AMAZING LOVE)

A - maz - ing love,__ how__ can__ it be__ that You,__ my King,__ would die__ for me?__

__ A - maz - ing love,__ I____ know__ it's true,__

it's my joy__ to hon - or You.__ In all__ I do, I'll hon - or You.__

Words and Music by BILLY JAMES FOOTE
© 1999 WORSHIPTOGETHER.COM SONGS (ASCAP)
Admin. by EMI CMG PUBLISHING
All Rights Reserved   Used by Permission

SING TO THE KING

Sing   to____   the   King   who____   is

com - ing____ to reign.__ Glo - ry__ to

Je - sus,__ the Lamb that__ was slain.__

Words and Music by BILLY JAMES FOOTE
© 2003 WORSHIPTOGETHER.COM SONGS (ASCAP) and sixsteps Music (ASCAP)
Admin. by EMI CMG PUBLISHING
All Rights Reserved   Used by Permission

TRACK 82 Demo TRACK 83 Play-Along

CHAPTER 8: READING A SONG CHART

If you ever plan to jam with other musicians or maybe play in the band at church, you'll find it very helpful to know how to read a song chart. A song chart is basically a road map through an entire song. It usually consists of chord symbols, lyrics, and the vocal melody, although it will occasionally feature instrumental phrases as well. With practice and experience, you'll eventually reach the point where, with the aid of a song chart, you'll be able to convincingly fake your way through a song that you've never even heard.

While I could list the new items that you'll see in a chart, it's probably easier to learn by seeing them in action. So we'll look at a complete chart first, and then I'll go through and explain each element. The items described in detail will be marked in the chart with a circled number.

Let's take a look at "Lord, Reign in Me." Look the song over, but don't listen to the audio yet.

TRACK 84 Demo   **TRACK 85** Play-Along

LORD, REIGN IN ME

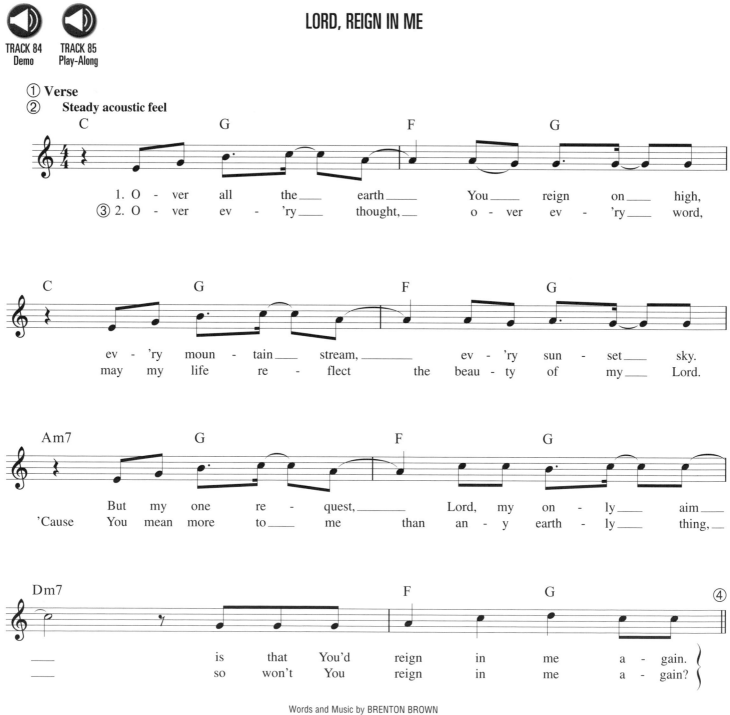

Words and Music by BRENTON BROWN
© 1998 VINEYARD SONGS (UK/EIRE)
Admin. in North America by MUSIC SERVICES o/b/o VINEYARD MUSIC GLOBAL INC.
All Rights Reserved   Used by Permission

36

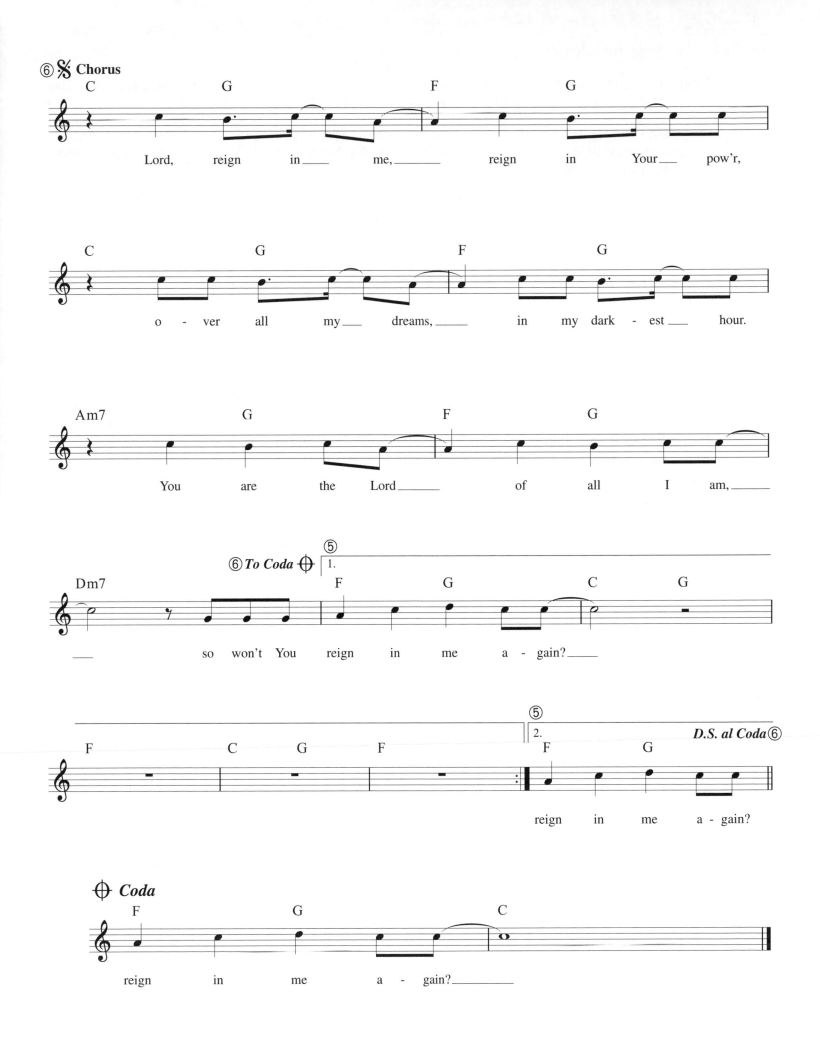

Now let's cover the important elements.

1. **Section Names:** Many song charts will delineate the different sections of the song (verse, chorus, bridge, etc.). This is helpful for quick reference when someone says something like, "Let's take it from the chorus."

2. **Tempo/Style marking:** This lets you know how the song should be played in terms of style and tempo. Sometimes this will have a specific BPM (beats per minute) number, while other times (as it is here) it will use a descriptive phrase to suggest the proper feel.

3. **Additional Lyrics:** The numbers in front of the lyrics tell you which verse to sing first, which to sing second, etc. Sometimes, instead of having the extra verses written out beneath the first verse along with the music, you'll see "see additional lyrics" written after the "2." (or "3." or maybe "4."). This tells you that all of the extra verses are numbered and written out (kind of like a poem) at the end of the chart.

4. **Double Bar Line:** A double bar line is used in most song charts at the end of a section. Here the double bar separates the verse from the chorus.

5. **First and Second Endings:** These are used in conjunction with repeat signs as a way of avoiding having to write out a bunch of common musical material. They're used when most of the section repeats, but things change at the very end.

   In this instance, you would play through the song until you run into the repeat sign :‖ . Since you don't have an opening repeat sign (the one with the two dots on the right of the lines), you return to the very beginning of the song and play it again. This time, however, once you reach the measure where the bracketed first ending begins ⌐1.⌐ , you skip over to where the bracketed second ending begins ⌐2.⌐ and play from there.

6. **D.S. al Coda:** There are two parts to this phrase. "D.S." stands for *dal segno*, which is Italian for *from the sign*. When you reach this direction, you go back and start from the sign (𝄋). The second part, "al Coda," means *to the coda*. After going back and starting from the sign, you play up until you see the "To Coda" indication ⊕. At this point, you skip ahead to the bottom of the page to the section called the "Coda." It will have a symbol that looks like a circle with crosshairs. In this case, after you start from the Coda, you just play those last two measures and you're done! (Note: You always ignore the "To Coda" direction until you're instructed to look for it.)

After you've studied these directions a bit and are ready to test yourself, listen to the recording and try to follow along. If you get lost, go back and re-read the explanations. It may take a few times through the song, but soon you'll be navigating like a pro!

ADDITIONAL ITEMS

Though "Lord, Reign in Me" contains most of the commonly-seen elements of a song chart, there are others items you may run into as well.

D.C.: "D.C." stands for *da capo*, which means *from the head*. This tells you to go back and start from the very beginning of the song. "D.C." can be used sometimes in place of "D.S." So you may see "D.C. al Coda" or "D.C. al fine" (see below).

al fine: This basically means *to the finish* or *to the end*. You'll see it usually either after "D.S." or "D.C." After returning to the specified point (either the sign or the beginning of the song), you play through until you see the word "Fine." When you reach that, you stop; the song's over! As with the "To Coda" direction, you ignore "Fine" until you're instructed to look for it.

APPENDIX

USING A CAPO

A *capo* is a device that clamps onto the neck of a guitar, barring across the strings at whichever fret you choose. In essence, it becomes a moveable nut, allowing you to raise the pitches of all the open strings evenly without having to retune the guitar. There are a few different types of capos available, with the most popular being the "quick-change" type. A "poor man's" capo can even be fashioned from a rubber band and a pen or pencil if you're flat broke!

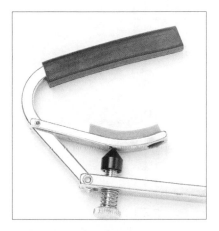

Capos are great for adjusting the key of a song to better fit a vocal range. If you know a song with the chords C, G, Am, and Em, for instance, but the melody is too high or low for you to sing, you can try using a capo on different frets until the range is better for your voice.

Listen to the audio. First you'll hear C, G, Am, and Em chords played normally (without a capo). Then you'll hear those same chords played with a capo on the third fret. The same thing is being played, but it sounds higher!

TRACK 86

CARE AND MAINTENANCE

With the proper care, a guitar is an instrument that can last a lifetime and beyond. Compared to many other things, caring for your guitar is a breeze! Here are a few ways to keep your instrument looking and sounding great.

1. **Use common sense**: Don't leave your guitar laying on the floor where it can be tripped over, trampled on, etc. And don't leave it leaning precariously against a door, a desk, or anything else that's not a guitar stand. The law of averages ensures that if you continue to do this, it *will* eventually take a nasty fall.

2. **Wash your hands!**: Try to get into the habit of washing your hands every time before you play. This will not only keep excessive oil and dirt off your instrument, but it will also tremendously extend the life of your strings.

3. **Power off**: When dealing with an electric guitar, make all cord connections and disconnections with the equipment turned off. This protects your speakers from possibly-damaging "pop" noises.

A WORD ON PRACTICING

When first starting out on the guitar, you're likely to progress very quickly, and it will all seem very exciting. Eventually, you'll most likely reach your first plateau, and it will seem as though you've stopped improving. When this happens, many players stop practicing and begin playing only once a week or so, only to maintain their current level. This is a big mistake if you want to continue to improve.

It is *always* better to practice more frequently for shorter periods of time than it is to cram one mega-practice session into seven hours on a Saturday. Even thirty minutes a day (which only totals three and a half hours) would be much more effective than seven hours on one day. In order to stay interested with such frequent practice, you need to make an effort to keep your sessions fresh. Try learning new songs, new chords, new scales, etc. Simply playing the same thing over and over again is a surefire way to get into a rut, and a rut can cause some players to quit altogether.

COMMON CHORDS

Here are chord grids for the most common chords you're likely to encounter:

D

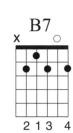

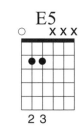

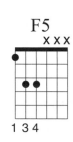

F

B7

E5

F5

G5

A5

B5

C5

D5